First published in Great Britain in 1997 by
Brockhampton Press,
20 Bloomsbury Street,
London WC1B 3QA.
A member of the Hodder Headline Group.

This series of little gift books was made by Frances Banfield,
Penny Clarke, Clive Collins, Jack Cooper, Nick Diggory,
John Dunne, David Goodman, Paul Gregory, Douglas Hall,
Lucinda Hawksley, Dicky Howett, Dennis Hovell, Helen Johnson,
C. M. Lee, John Maxwell, Patrick McCreeth, Morse Modaberi,
Sonya Newland, Anne Newman, Terry Price, Mike Seabrook,
Nigel Soper, Karen Sullivan, Nick Wells and Matt Weyland.

ISBN 1 86019 557 1

A copy of the CIP data is available from the
British Library upon request.

Produced for Brockhampton Press by Flame Tree Publishing,
a part of The Foundry Creative Media Company Limited,
The Long House, Antrobus Road, Chiswick, London W4 5HY.

Printed and bound in Italy by L.E.G.O. Spa.

The Funny Book of
WORK

Selected by
Karen Sullivan

Cartoons by

BROCKHAMPTON PRESS

This woman is headstrong, obstinate and
dangerously self-opinionated.
*Report by a personnel officer at ICI,
rejecting Mrs Thatcher for a job in 1948*

The trouble with unemployment is that the minute
you wake up in the morning you're on the job.
Slappy White

The volume of paper expands to
fill the available briefcases.
Jerry Brown

Executive ability is deciding quickly and getting
somebody else to do the work.
J. G. Pollard

"*Handy that — him being a mechanic . . . .*"

"It's on again . . . ?"

8

The brain is a wonderful organ; it starts working the moment you get up in the morning and does not stop until you get to the office.

Robert Frost

No king on earth is as safe in his job as a Trade Union official. There is only one thing that can get him sacked; and that is drink. Not even that, as long as he doesn't actually fall down.

George Bernard Shaw

Business is so bad that even the shoplifters have stopped coming.

Anonymous

The only way to succeed is to make people hate you.

Josef von Sternberg

A molehill man is a pseudo-busy executive who comes to work at 9 a.m. and finds a molehill on his desk. He has until 5 p.m. to make this molehill into a mountain. An accomplished molehill man will often have his mountain finished before lunch.

Fred Allen

It's true hard work never killed anybody, but I figure, why take the chance?

Ronald Reagan

It is too difficult to think nobly when one thinks only of earning a living.

Jean-Jacques Rousseau

It's just a job. Grass grows, birds fly, waves pound the sand. I beat people up.

Mohammed Ali

"... and on a clear day, you can see them clearing
the site for the next phase of development ...."

The human race is faced with a cruel choice:
work or daytime television.

Anonymous

In a hierarchy, every employee tends
to rise to his level of incompetence.

Laurence J. Peters

Work is a necessity for man.
Man invented the alarm clock.

Pablo Picasso

Foreman: Can you brew a good cup of tea?
Applicant: Yes.
Foreman: Can you drive a stacker truck?
Applicant: Why? Is it a big teapot?

The Huge Joke Book

There's always one smartarse in every batch."

An executive is a person who has mastered the art of shuffling Credit and Blame back and forth between his In-Basket and his Out-Basket.

Anonymous

It's better to have a permanent income than be fascinating.

Oscar Wilde

I learned in business that you had to be very careful when you told somebody that's working for you to do something, because the chances were very high he'd do it. In government you don't have to worry about that.

George Shultz

Where do you complain about the complaints department?

Anonymous

Perpetual devotion to what a man calls his
business, is only to be sustained by perpetual
neglect of many other things.

Robert Louis Stevenson

By working faithfully eight hours a day
you may eventually get to be a boss and
work twelve hours a day.

Robert Frost

The big guns of business are usually those
who have never been fired.

Anonymous

The worst thing about retirement is having
to drink coffee in your own time.

Anonymous

"The team that compiled the index feel
that they should sign as well . . . ."

The two tradesmen of the town met.
'Trade's bad,' said one man. 'I heard that your
factory burned down today.'
'Sssh,' said the second. 'It's tomorrow.'
The Huge Joke Book

If you can't get a job as a pianist in a
brothel you become a royal reporter.
Max Hastings

The greatest analgesic, soporific, stimulant,
tranquilliser, narcotic, and to some extent even
antibiotic — in short, the closest thing to a genuine
panacea — known to medical science is work.
Thomas Szasz

No one hates his job so heartily as a farmer.
H. L. Mencken

Work is of two kinds: first, altering the position of matter at or near the earth's surface relative to other matter; second, telling other people to do it.

Bertrand Russell

He [Robert Benchley] and I had an office so tiny that an inch smaller and it would have been adultery.

Dorothy Parker

Work is the curse of the drinking classes.

Oscar Wilde

The important thing about your lot in life is whether you use it for building or parking.

Reader's Digest

A tremendous number of people in America
work very hard at something that bores them.
Even a rich man thinks he has to go down
to the office every day. Not because he likes it
but because he can't think of anything else to do.

Anonymous

A businessman had three trays on his desk marked:
'In', 'Out' and 'LBW'.
A client asked him what was the meaning of LBW,
and the businessman explained: 'Oh, that means,
"Let the blighters wait!"'

The Huge Joke Book

Angry employer: You should have
been here at nine o'clock.
Late employee: Why, what happened?

Matthew Mark Luke and John
are Data Banks to count upon —
4 computers round my bed
2 at my foot 2 at my head
1 to watch 1 to play
& 2 to file my soul away
Matthew Mark Luke and John
guard my cards when I am gone.
*Anthony Haden-Guest, '**Computaprayer**'*

When I give a man an office, I watch him carefully
to see whether he is swelling or growing.
Woodrow Wilson

The boss is usually the only one who watches
the clock during the coffee break.
Anonymous

"*Actually our founder was small, fat and bald.
This is how we felt our founder should have looked . . . .*"

"I just don't feel you're taking
this job seriously, Dawson!"

It is easier to appear worthy of a position one does not hold, than of the office which one fills.

François, Duc de la Rochefoucauld

I'm tired of Love: I'm still more tired of Rhyme.
But Money gives me pleasure all the time.

Hilaire Belloc

He is something in the City
And, as if that were a pity,
The suit he wears is sombre black or grey.

*Charles Blackburn Owen, **'Underground Press'***

Filing cabinet: Useful container where things can be lost alphabetically.

Anonymous

Oh to be in banking
Now that April's here!
And celebrate a spanking,
Profitable year!
Bertie Ramsbottom, **'The Bankers'**

Work with some men is as
besetting a sin as idleness.
Samuel Butler

Boss: Did you take any messages while I was out?
Secretary: No, are any of them missing?

It's no go my honey love,
it's no go my poppet;
Work your hands from day to day,
the winds will blow the profit.
Louis MacNeice, **'Bagpipe Music'**

27

Before you have an argument with the boss, take a good look at both sides — her side and the outside.

Anonymous

This high official, all allow
Is grossly overpaid.
There wasn't any Board; and now
There isn't any trade.

Sir A. P. Herbert, 'On the President of the Board of Trade'

Work expands so as to fill the time available for its completion.

C. Northcote Parkinson

I yield to no one in my admiration for the office as a social centre, but it's no place to get any work done.

Katherine Whitehorn

"It's about my friend, doctor . . . ."

"This is actually a fake. The original is downstairs
in the canteen having his tea-break . . . ."

Angry employer: Why are you late
again this morning?
Young typist: I overslept.
Angry employer: You mean you sleep at home too?

Ambition often puts Men upon doing
the meanest offices; so climbing is performed
in the same position with creeping.
Jonathan Swift

Who first invented Work — and tied the free
And holy-day rejoicing spirit down
To the ever-haunting importunity of business?
Charles Lamb

Business is so quiet you can
hear the overheads piling up.
Anonymous

At an international sales exhibition, one
British salesman turned to another and asked:
'How are you faring today?'
'Quite well,' replied the other salesman.
'I've picked up lots of useful information,
followed up a number of promising leads,
renewed relationships with a number of potential
customers and made a lot of valuable new contacts.'
'So have I,' responded the first salesman.
'I haven't sold anything yet, either.'

The Huge Joke Book

Where the whole man is involved there is no work.
Work begins with the division of labour.

Marshall McLuhan

Why should I let the toad work
Squat on my life?

Philip Larkin, 'Toads'

*"If you don't mind, sir,
I'd prefer to serve someone younger."*

"Bad news, I'm afraid —
you've got rising sponge . . . ."

34

Lord Finchley tried to mend the Electric Light
Himself. It struck him dead: and serve him right!
It is the business of the wealthy man
To give employment to the artisan.

*Hilaire Belloc, '**Lord Finchley**'*

Of the professions, it may be said that soldiers are
becoming too popular, parsons too lazy, physicians
too mercenary, and lawyers too powerful.

Charles Caleb Cotton

The salary of the chief executive of the large
corporation is not a market award for achievement.
It is frequently in the nature of a warm personal
gesture by the individual to himself.

John Kenneth Galbraith

It is not real work unless you would
rather be doing something else.
J. M. Barrie

After all, it is hard to master both life
and work equally well. So if you are bound
to fake one of them, it had better be life.
Joseph Brodsky

I am afraid that the pleasantness of an employment
does not always evince its propriety.
Jane Austen, **Sense and Sensibility**

Nothing makes a man so selfish as work.
George Bernard Shaw

"George, I've never pried —
but just what do you do on the night shift?"

I suspect that American workers have
come to lack a work ethic. They do not
live by the sweat of their brow.
Kiichi Miyazawa

I am a young executive.
No cuffs than mine are cleaner;
I have a Slimline brief-case
and I use the firm's Cortina.
John Betjeman, 'Executive'

But the difficulties go to understand,
And the difficultest job a man can do,
Is to come it brave and meek with thirty bob a week,
And feel that that's the proper thing for you.
John Davidson, 'Thirty Bob a Week'

"Look everybody, he gave me a tip! No more waiting on tables for me — now I can open my own restaurant!"

"My brother and I would prefer
'Digby & Digby' if you don't mind."

Policy is the people you work with.
William Gaskill

I always laugh at my boss's jokes. It doesn't
give me a lift but it might give me a raise.

Anonymous

I trod, where fools alone may tread,
Who speak what's better left unsaid,
The day I asked the boss his view
On what I was supposed to do.

*Bertie Ramsbottom, **'The Job Description'***

It is wonderful when a calculation is made,
how little the mind is actually employed in
the discharge of any profession.

Samuel Johnson

All jobs should be open to everybody, unless they
actually require a penis or vagina.
Florynce Kennedy

This is the world in which he lives:
Four walls, a desk, a swivel chair,
A doorway with no door to close,
Vents to bring in air.
*Dana Gioia, '**The Man in the Open Doorway**'*

Let us be grateful to Adam, our benefactor.
He cut us out of the 'blessing' of idleness
and won for us the 'curse' of labour.
Mark Twain

Cultivating a friend in business
Is tightrope walking in a gale.
*Harry Newman, '**Business Friends**'*

"Dobson! Any surprise value in having a security camera is lost if you ask them to smile!"

A commuter is one who never knows how a show comes out because he has to leave early to catch a train to get him back to the country in time to catch a train to bring him back to the city.

Ogden Nash, **The Commuter's Song**

Clearly the most unfortunate people are those who must do the same thing over and over again, every minute, or perhaps twenty to the minute. They deserve the shortest hours and the highest pay.

John Kenneth Galbraith

Bit by bit and byte by byte
My messages do flow;
They come by electronic flight
For Cupid's far too slow.

Quentin de la Bedoyere, 'A Valentine for Christmas'

People hate work. If work was so bloody great, the rich would have reserved more of it for themselves.

Frank Dobson MP, after a pious pronouncement on the dignity of labour by a hugely wealthy Tory in the House of Commons

Work! Labour the *aspergas me* of life; the one great sacrament of humanity from which all other things flow — security, leisure, joy, art, literature, even divinity itself.

Sean O'Casey

One of the symptoms of approaching nervous breakdown is the belief that one's work is terribly important. If I were a medical man, I should prescribe a holiday to any patient who considered his work important.

Bertrand Russell

*"He's feeling terribly unwanted —
nobody's paged him in days."*

The Business true-believer's Shrine
Is something called 'The Bottom Line'.
Bertie Ramsbottom

I don't want any yes-men around me.
I want everybody to tell me the truth,
even if it costs them their jobs.
Samuel Goldwyn

Well, we can't stand around here doing
nothing, people will think we are workmen.
Spike Milligan, **The Goon Show**

Unionism seldom, if ever, uses such power as it has
to ensure better work; almost always it devotes a
large part of that power to safeguarding bad work.
H. L. Mencken, **Prejudices**

I like the job; it's the work I hate.

Anonymous

Nowher so bisy a man as he ther nas,
And yet he semed bisier than he was.

Geoffrey Chaucer

If your son has a nose,
send him out to Grasse.
You know it makes scents.

Anonymous

Minister of Labour: The workers of
Freedonia are demanding shorter hours.
Firefly (Groucho Marx): Very well,
we'll give them shorter hours. We'll start by
cutting their lunch hour to twenty minutes.

Screenplay for Duck Soup

The difference between my company and a cactus
is that the cactus has the pricks on the outside.
Graffito

He was fired with enthusiasm because
he wasn't fired with enthusiasm.
Anonymous

My brother-in-law: I wish he would learn a trade,
so we'd know what kind of work he was out of.
Henny Youngman

Galbraith's Law states that anyone who says
he won't resign four times will.
John Kenneth Galbraith

"Do us a favour and slip this on for a while —
you're on TV . . . ."

So much of what we call management consists
of making it difficult for people to work.

Peter Drucker

When you see what some girls marry, you realize
how much they must hate to work for a living.

Helen Rowland

A clergyman is one who feels himself called
upon to live without working at the expense
of the rascals who work to live.

Voltaire

1st person: I left because my boss
used disgraceful language to me.
2nd person: What did he say?
1st person: He said, 'You're fired!'

Of all the businesses, by far,
Consultancy's the most bizarre!

Bertie Ramsbottom, 'The Business Consultant'

*"Sometimes I long for a break-in,
just to relieve the monotony . . . ."*

*"Emergency! Emergency!
This is an emergency!"*

I am a friend of the working man, and I would
rather be his friend than be one.

Clarence Darrow, **US lawyer**

Good career move.

RCA Victor executive, on being told of Elvis Presley's death

Work is work if you're paid to do it, and it's
pleasure if you pay to be allowed to do it.

Finley Peter Dunne

The world is full of willing people: some willing
to work, the rest willing to let them.

Robert Frost

I like work. I could watch it all day.

Anonymous

"You just can't take your mind off
the office for a moment, can you!"

I have never liked working.
To me a job is an invasion of privacy.
Danny McGoorty

I must have, in a long life, ground through between
a hundred and fifty thousand and two hundred
thousand hours of perfectly useless work.
Leonard Woolf, **The Journey not the Arrival Matters**

Most people are too busy working
to earn any money.
Anonymous

After all, the best part of a holiday is
perhaps not so much to be resting yourself,
as to see all the other fellows busy working.
Kenneth Grahame, **The Wind in the Willows**

1st person: How many people work in your office?

2nd person: Oh, about half.

The Huge Joke Book

*"We couldn't think of a suitable retirement gift,
so we've bought you a plot just here . . . ."*

An office party is not, as is sometimes supposed, the Managing Director's chance to kiss the tea-girl. It is the tea-girl's chance to kiss the Managing Director (however bizarre an ambition this may seem to anyone who has seen the Managing Director face on). Bringing down the mighty from their seats is an agreeable and necessary pastime, but no one supposes that the mighty, having struggled so hard to get seated, will enjoy the dethronement.

Katharine Whitehorn

I used to be a white-collar worker but I had to quit — the collar got dirty.

Anonymous

George goes to sleep at a bank from ten to four each day, except Saturdays, when they wake him up and put him outside at two.

*Jerome K. Jerome, **Three Men in a Boat***

Acknowledgements:

The Publishers wish to thank everyone who gave permission to reproduce the quotes in this book. Every effort has been made to contact the copyright holders, but in the event that an oversight has occurred, the publishers would be delighted to rectify any omissions in future editions of this book. Children's quotes printed courtesy of Herne Hill School; Dorothy Parker quotes from *The Best of Dorothy Parker*, first published by Methuen in 1952, reprinted by Gerald Duckworth & Co., © Dorothy Parker, 1956, 1957, 1958, 1959, renewed; Robert Frost from *The Poetry of Robert Frost*, reprinted by permission of Jonathan Cape, the Estate of Robert Frost and Peter A. Gilbert, North Hampshire, USA © Robert Frost; G. K. Chesterton reprinted courtesy of Methuen and Dodd Mead, copyright renewed; *The Huge Joke Book* edited by Kevin Goldstein-Jackson, Ernest Ford and A. C. H. Newman, Elliott Right Way Books © A. C. H. Newman, Ernest Ford and Elliott Right Way Books; Ogden Nash, from *Verses from 1929 on* reprinted by permission of Curtis Brown, Ltd. Copyright © 1942 by Ogden Nash, renewed; Hilaire Belloc reprinted from *The Complete Verse of Hilaire Belloc*, by permission of Peters Fraser & Dunlop Group Ltd; Philip Larkin, first verse of *Toads*, reprinted courtesy of Faber & Faber Limited; Kenneth Grahame, *The Wind in the Willows*, reprinted courtesy of Methuen Children's Books, text copyright The University Chest, Oxford, under the Berne Convention, copyright renewed; J. M. Barrie reprinted courtesy of Great Ormond Street Hospital.